Follow This Blood to Find a Dead Thing

This book is nothing short of an epiphany. It takes you to the raw edges of existence, where nature's beauty and our fear of losing her blend into a powerful sense of dread and reverence. I also found myself profoundly connected to its exploration of queerness as it navigates love, loss, and survival within a world that can feel both breathtaking and brutal. Every poem and tale felt like an invitation to reflect on my place in this vast, fragile world, and it moved me to consider the depth of my own connection to our planet, the creatures here with us, and all the other humans who have impacted me over the years—for better or for worse. This collection sparked emotions I didn't know I was holding onto and walked me from my yearning to live a brilliant beautiful life to all the fears that I suppress and run from on a daily basis. A true tour de force of the emotions we all need to feel and engage with to heal. This is a book I'll return to again and again, always finding tears glistening down my face when I get to the penultimate poem from the author and the oracle.

—TIMOTHY ARLISS OBRIEN
author of *Wild Queer Magic*

In *Follow This Blood to Find a Dead Thing*, Charles K. Carter offers a meditative—often haunting—exploration into the heartfelt and heart-breaking complexities and contradictions of how we live in nature and with fellow creatures. He offers his poems and stories as a shaman might use parables to show us the ways of our wanton destruction and trauma on a global and personal level but also the healing and restorative powers of the heart and finding our ancestral roots deep in the earth. "We are lonely hunters scavenging the fluid boundary. / We feel the current within ourselves. / We want to dive into each other because we are single drops of the same vast sea." These are inventive, beautiful poems and stories told with a soft but powerful voice. And as we seemingly race headlong in extinction and a human-centric existence, these sublime and deeply honest pieces do offer hope and shed light on the untamed wildness of the world within and without.

—SARAH ROHRS

Queer questions of nature, evolution, and family riddle these essential poems by Charles K. Carter in which decay is sexy, and the oracle gives our world a childless ending instead of a new, unwanted Eden. Apocalypse and ecstasy mix. If you *Follow This Blood*, as the title poem wants you to do, expect to find crows hunting baby squirrels and blue octopi strangling their mates. But these poems don't merely disturb. They agitate as much as they educate us about queerness thriving in every branch and web.

—MICHAEL WALSH
editor of *Queer Nature*

Follow This Blood to Find a Dead Thing

poems and tales by
CHARLES K. CARTER

Fernwood
PRESS

Follow This Blood to Find a Dead Thing

Fernwood Press
Newberg, Oregon
www.fernwoodpress.com

Printed in the United States of America

Cover and page design: Mareesa Fawver Moss
Cover art: "maneater" by Claire Quelle
Author photo: Brandon Carter

ISBN 978-1-59498-200-2

for Bella, Jasmine, & Stevie
—the most human of us all

Contents

The Oracle

How will the world end?
I ask her. *Will we all blow*
up in a nuke's blast?

No, no, she replies.
It will be slow. Some will burn.
Some drown. Most will starve.

I.

Conversation with a Grandmother

I'm sorry for the gnats, I say,
swatting at one, noticing another one infiltrating the dining room.

Never apologize for gnats or flies, dear.
That simply means there is life in your home, she says.

It can be a sign of death, too,
I reply.

They are the same thing.

A Trip to the Zoo

Penguins!

And before his father could follow, Gideon ran off in the direction of the enclosure.

He watched one short penguin waddle over to another and slap it with its flipper.

Gideon laughed.

The slapper then waddled over to the pool's edge and dove into the water.

> A speaker near the enclosure spoke, *Adelie penguins were originally found right here in Antarctica, long before humans settled here. They lived on krill, a type of small fish, now extinct, found underneath the ancient ice glaciers.*

The penguin swam fast around the pool.

Daddy, look!

His father was talking to some woman in a summer dress and not paying him much for attention.

Gideon frowned and turned back to the penguin, bringing his face to the glass, watching the penguin dart back and forth, spinning under the water.

> *Male and female Adelie penguins are hard to tell apart. Both contain white front sides and black back sides. You may also notice white spots around their eyes. The males would build nests for their mates by gathering rocks, sometimes stealing from their neighbors. They would ...*

Come on, Gideon, it's time to go.

But I want to stay and watch the penguins.

The zoo is going to close soon.

Gideon frowned.

The father knelt down beside his child. *You know, we can watch penguins on the TV at home, too.*

It's not the same. Gideon pouted, crossing his arms.

The father chewed on his bottom lip, thinking of a bargaining tool.

> The speaker continued, *As glacial ice melted, the Adelie penguin's food sources dwindled and the last members of the species went extinct over seventy-five years ago. Stop by our gift shop on your way out today to pick up your very own Adelie penguin hologram just like the ones you see here in the zoo!*

The father's eyes brightened. *What if I get you a penguin from the gift shop and then you can watch TV at home with him?*

Gideon's eyes beamed, and his mouth dropped open. He nodded, smiling.

The father took his child's hand. They began to walk away. Gideon took one more look back at the penguin enclosure before it flickered off for the night.

Birds

Birds are the spirits of our loved ones returned:
the mourning dove's coo-coos of gossiping old aunts

and soothing chirps of your grandmother's song,
the parrot's war paint mimics that of your mother,

the cardinal rare and stunning but surely your brother
dressed in the blood they drained from his tattooed veins—

but then there is the crow, your father's deadly caw,
pecking at the seeds he dropped in your pretty little skull.

You morphed into a skilled archer, a huntress,
slaying him again and again.

He comes back, higher up the aviary chain;
some demon must have it in for you, sweet girl

fed by nectar and sugar water, trying to erase the bitter
grip he has on your synapses, your paranoid flight,

your panicked heartbeat, *beat, beat,* beating so fast.
He returns a falcon. An eagle. A mythological roc.

He plucks the huntress up in his talons, takes her away,
drops her off the edge of the earth,

erasing his only sweet mark on this world,
making his own hummingbird daughter his prey.

The Pride

Mamma is

a lioness,

a huntress,

a provider,

tracking down

coupons

and garage sales

to keep us fed

and clothed,

safe beside her.

Papa is

a lazy lion,

catting around all night,

sleeping all

damn day,

taking

voluntary layoff

every time

it comes

his way.

On Being Twelve,
Riding a Bike at Summer's End

August—
when the grasshoppers jump around
spitting tar from their mouths.

Follow This Blood

Like a criminal in an action movie,
my anxiety moves in shadow,

jumps through the window and stalks.
Instead of running away from the good guys,

it is rifle-ready, chasing me.
Just like in a movie, it doesn't even flinch

after going through the window,
it easily hops over the porch rail

and glides effortlessly down the street
even as glass and rock and pavement tear at its feet.

Like a hunter tracking its game,
follow this blood to find a dead thing.

Spider

> "Loneliness has been estimated to shorten a person's life by 15 years, equivalent in impact to smoking 15 cigarettes per day."
> —*Scientific American*

The spider has been here every day for a week.
Sometimes she's in the corner of the ceiling,
sometimes on the shower wall or on the mirror's face.
She is always there, and I greet her with a *Hello, friend.*

But now she's gone.
She's gone, and I don't know how to mourn this minor change
in my day-to-day without looking like a complete fool.

Loneliness will trap a fool under a glass,
silencing their cries for help.

Blooming

The orchid Drakaea glyptodon
grows to look like a female wasp
attracting male wasps to rub up against it,
tempting with sex only to spread its own genetics.

*

Gardenias
smell sweet to attract daytime pollinators.

*

Some flowers
are too bright
for the human eye to register.
We see white,
but the bees see
a lit-up Las Vegas Strip.

*

Petunias can shed
their own dead weight.

*

Many native prairie flowers grow close together
to help each other carry the weight of the world,
to help each other stand tall.

*

I, too, want to attract what I need,
cast off what I don't,
and just keep

rising.

S.O.S.

Ripples upon the surface
warn of trouble
far below.

II.

Question

Why do you write so
damn much about insects
and flying things? he asks.

Because I have a
recurring dream, one where
I have always flown.

A Place of Their Own

We'll take it! Ella turned to her husband and wrapped her arms around him. *A place of our own!*

Evan smiled and kissed her on the top of her head.

*

They almost immediately moved their belongings from their respective parents' homes—not that either one had much to start with. She went to buy paint while he set up the utilities. With each setup, he calculated their monthly budget in his head. The last stop was to register with the Mexico City Water Board.

He shifted his weight on his feet as he waited for the city worker to process the application. He read a faded sign:

> Parts of Mexico City sink
> an average of 1.5 m every year.
>
> DO YOUR PART TO CONSERVE!

You'll be on a budget of two hundred gallons of water per week at a cost of two hundred ninety-two pesos per week. Would you like to set up an auto payment?

Evan nodded.

*

They both met at the front door of their new home as if the stars had aligned for them to do so. *Mi amor!* He swept Ella off her feet, carrying her across the threshold.

*

They painted the living room sky blue and the kitchen canary yellow, the way she had always wanted. *It'll be like waking up to the sun every morning.*

But the sun comes up without the paint, he protested.

He knew this was a fight he would not win.

*

The bedroom stayed white with one of her original abstract paintings centered above the headboard—two sharp red lines running in opposite directions.

Magnifico! he proclaimed, playfully pulling her onto the bed, on top of him. She laughed. They kissed. They christened their new home with the passionate lovemaking that could only be made by a young couple starting off, the world full of possibility. The pale white moon fell upon their naked skin as they fell asleep that first night in their new home. *Their* home!

*

CITY STREETS CRUMBLING

MEXICO CITY – 13 JUNE 2046

Early Tuesday morning, at
approximately 3:00 AM, a
neighborhood south of Parque
de los Periodists Lustres
suffered from ground collapse.
Like earlier reported cases,
this incident was thought to
be caused by depleting under-
ground aquifers. The city
has been attempting to fill
these with recycled sewage
water to prevent further
damage, though the mayor
warns that these incidents
may become more commonplace.
Privada Zoquipa and Calle
1821 saw the most infra-
structure damage. Emergency
workers helped secure the area
and treat nearly a dozen in-
juries. Two deaths were confirmed:
newlyweds Evan and Ella (Gomez)
Flores.

I Don't Know If It Makes Me Feel Better or Worse That We Aren't the Only Ones

After my great-grandmother died,
it didn't take long for my great-grandfather
to follow his broken heart into the darkness.

Ducks tend to only mate for a season,
but they love so hard that sometimes
one will intentionally drown itself after losing a mate.

Snake

He's venom-ready,
flattening himself
and sneaking
under the door

into my happiness.

Taxonomy

My father was a willow tree.
Bark for ancient medicine.
Bark for chasing away pain.

My father was a willow tree.
Branch can also be called switch.

*

My father is poison ivy.
One leaf for his abandoned child,
one leaf for his abused daughter,
one leaf for his neglected mother—
three ugly leaves grow from his stem.

My aunt always said, *Leaves of three, let them be.*

*

My father is a Venus flytrap.
Always hungry.
Always searching.
Always ready to snap.

*

My father is a gympie-gympie,
also known as the "suicide plant."
He is a tree covered in poisonous needles.
One touch, and his acid burns.
His poison lingers in the body for years,
driving you insane,
driving you to wonder if it's really worth all of this pain.

*

My father is a corpse flower:
big, colorful, the center of attention,
smelling of rotting flesh.

*

I want to be a willow tree,
to rid myself of his crippling abuse and disease.

To heal, to shine, to *rise*.

Trophy

My first landlord had jowls like an old Walter Matthau
and walls covered in exotic animal carcasses.

I'm getting married and want to add my spouse to the lease.

Well. All right, he said. *What's her name?*

He, actually.

His eyes shifted to a blank space on his wall.
His eyes shined bright. Electric even.

Willful Ignorance:
A Gay Scavenger Hunt

anglerfish. Baboon. barn owl.

bearded dragon. bison. bonobo.

bowfly. box crab. brown bear.

brown rat. bUtterfly. caribou.

caT. chicken. chImpanzee.

cockroach. cow. crickeT.

desert tortoiSe. dog. dolphin.

dove. dragoNfly. elephant.

emu. fly. fOx. frog.

garTer snake. giraffe. goat.

horse. jumpiNg spider. koAla.

lion. locusT. mallard.

mite. moth. moUrning gecko.

orca. ostRich. panda.

penguin. rAccoon. rattlesnake.

raven. saLamander. salmon.

sparrow. toad. wasp.

water moccasin.

Hunted

I.

Last Saturday
a small bird flew into our broken window
and fell between the panes.

She was being hunted by a hawk.
When the hawk realized he was unable to grab her,
he flew to a nearby tree to perch and wait for her escape.

The little bird tried and cried to free herself,
but the space between the panes was too restricting
to permit liftoff, especially for a novice aviator.

My husband watched until the hawk flew off.
Then he went outside, grabbed a stick, and stuck it between
the window panes, creating an escape route.

He stepped back
and allowed her to hop up the twig
before finding sweet freedom in the autumn air.

II.

I am often trapped
by my own insecurities
hunting me down day after day.

And he is gentle.
He is kind.
He is reassuring butterfly kisses.

He gives me light-up emergency exit signs to his arms,
a way to crawl out of my own misery;
but I am too afraid to scale these tall fortress walls.

These walls were built to protect me,
to save me from any more hurt,
to shield me from any more shame.

I don't know how to tear them down.
I don't know if I can.
I don't know if I can.

Who Is More Evolved?

An ant, used to relying on her colony to survive,
will purposefully leave her home if she is infected with a disease.
She will wander alone.
She will choose to take her own life
instead of bringing harm to the ones she loves.

One of my coworkers
couldn't even be bothered to wear a mask for ten minutes in Walgreens
where she was panic-purchasing toilet paper
at the height of the pandemic.
Her comfort took privilege over her elderly neighbors' safety.

Interloper

I want to belong to this wilderness.
I want to enjoy full-day hikes
and camping in a tent, not in a camper that costs more than my house.
I walk the nature trail around this man-made lake
and I want to let the wind wash away my sorrows.
The tall grasses have turned the color of wheat in the fall's chill.
I smoke a cigarette a mile in.
I stamp the butt beneath my boot
before stuffing it in my hoodie pocket.
I'll properly dispose of it later.
I hear rustling in the trees.
There have been mountain lion sightings in the area.
My cousin told me that his dog ran one of these wild cats off.
I pick up a large stick and hold it close—
just in case.
I walk in circles from time to time
nearly jumping out of these thick bones at birds rustling in the trees.
Then I stop in my tracks.
I pause and think
what a marvelous way it would be to go.
I drop the stick,
turn my back to the rustling foliage,
and keep walking on.
I want to find a way to belong in this wilderness.
Even if it is to feed its beasts of prey.

III.

Question

*Why do you write so
much about whales and swimming
things?* he questions me.

*Because I have this
recurring dream
where I am always drowning.*

Looting

The problem with looting in floodwater is that floodwater rarely stands still. That's why he always anchors himself to something: a fence post, a door handle, even heavy furniture will do in a pinch. Another thing to keep in mind is to travel light. Wear water-wicking clothing but not layers. He learned very quickly that everything gets heavier in rushing water. When she was still alive, he remembered holding her in the pool on their honeymoon: she felt weightless in his palms, her gold chain glistening in the sun, her skin glowing bronze. How deceiving still waters can be. There is no time for sitting still in moving water. He learned to be quick and efficient.

The problem with looting floodwaters in the Midwest is that there's no diving equipment readily available—so he had to make do with what he had: nothing.

He conditioned himself to hold his breath for a good five or six minutes. He always sets a four-minute timer on his digital watch. He hopes the air is just above his head, but that hasn't always been the case.

The china hutch will do, he thinks, tying himself to the handle.

Most days, he looks for things to pawn to eat. To get by. But on this day, he's in search of something in particular. This is personal.

He swims for the bedroom. Down the hall. To the left.

He knew this place.

It isn't in the nightstand or the dresser. He struggles with the wardrobe door, pressure built within its chamber. When he's finally able to power it open, he checks the box on the bottom right.

He knew this place.

The digital watch starts to blink green, the sound muffled and lost in the slosh of the ever-moving water.

He looks up but there is no up but ceiling.

He sets a one-minute timer, certain he can find what he needs before it goes off.

He makes his way to the bathroom. *Maybe it's in here.*

The watch silently sounds again.

He sighs the best sigh he can underwater and grabs the door frame, pushing himself back into the hallway, back toward the china hutch to free his tether. As another type of water fills his eyes, he notices a glimmer in the living room, a gold chain glistening.

His eyes grow wide. His hand reaches for the glow.

A rumble shakes the house and the far wall gives way, releasing rushing water to stir more chaos in this place. The china cabinet plunges forward, pinning him down to the floor.

As the carbon dioxide in his bloodstream builds, his arm still reaches for the gold chain. He is reaching, reaching for her.

The water keeps rushing.

The chain keeps gleaming.

The watch keeps blinking green.

Resilience

It is near the water's edge
you will find beautiful things growing

—so walk with me,
you beautiful creature,
across this great green Earth.

*

Though survival may be tough
and thriving even tougher yet,
there is resilience
birthed into every one of our cells.
We can look over our shoulders
and always find connection
and strength
in the natural world that surrounds us,
the mountains holding up the sky.

*

We are out of rhythm with our breath,
Always trying to create our own luck,
Deep breath in.　　　Take in the scent of pines.
Deep breath out.　　Let that lightness you feel spread like
　　　　　　　　　　seeds of hope.
We are out of touch; our focus is lost.

*

Our vision is blurred, beautiful one.
By imaginary limits and boundaries, we cage ourselves.
We are simply beasts with inflated egos.
There is no border that separates you from me.
There is no hierarchy that separates you from the elk.
There is no separation.
There is no separation.
There is no separation.

Only oneness.

Only love.

Love is everywhere you look on this Earth.
Love is what makes the Earth spin.
Love is what makes the Earth.
Love is what makes you.
Love is what makes.
Love is.

Wild Waters

We once rose from the sea like giants.

They say sixty percent of the human body is made up of water.
This is why there is such a deep stirring within that pulls us to
the water's edge.

We are lonely hunters scavenging the fluid boundary.

We feel the current within ourselves.
We want to dive into each other because we are single drops of
the same vast sea.

This is why we find comfort in the taste of our own tears and in
that of our lovers' salt.

Blessing

It is easy to feel small, my love.

You are not a blue whale calf
that packs on two hundred fifty pounds per day.
You are not a cow growing thirteen times its birth weight in its
first year.
German Shepherds grow seventy times their birth weight.

Sometimes our courage grows like a baby kangaroo,
less than a gram at birth, so small in the palm of one's hand,
but it grows to a modest six pounds by the time it jumps out of
the pouch.
And that is only the beginning, my love. It grows bigger yet.

It is easy to feel insignificant, my love.

A cactus only grows up to one inch a year.
Though they are as resilient as you are,
you are not a prickly thing.
You are a sunflower, standing tall.
Some varieties grow up to fourteen feet in one season.
Bamboo grows one hundred thirty feet in a season,
and I hope you grow confidence at an alarming rate,
that people look at you and see your might,
but even the mighty oaks and the weeping willows
only grow about four feet each in their first years.
It's okay to grow slow, my love, as long as you keep growing.

The bald eagles that nest in those mighty oaks
start off at only three-and-a-half ounces
before reaching a mature fourteen pounds in a matter of weeks.
It's okay to grow slow, my love, as long as you keep going.
Your development isn't on a timeline.
Just water your spirits, my love.
Feed your heart, my love, with greens and sunlight and you will grow.

Self-love starts off small, but it quickly grows wings.

Willful Ignorance

I saw a crow chasing a baby squirrel today,
nipping at its discolored tail.

I've never seen this before.
I thought crows were scavengers,

doing their part to hasten the decay.
I didn't know they could murder.

I didn't think they craved warm, fresh blood.
And maybe I don't know crows too well,

and I'm okay not looking up the truth.
I'm okay living with my fantasy,

thinking crows are noble and not dastardly;
that the world isn't after everything that is soft.

When She Shines

I think I would laugh if I were watching a western set in the rural
   American Midwest,
and a flock of bright green birds with bright yellow heads flew by.
I would find such a laughable error in filmmaking unforgivable.

The truth is, I don't know what the world was like in Iowa in the 1860s.
But the Carolina parakeet did exist in the heartland.
Its bright colors could be seen in the skies during that time.

It's hard to imagine something shining so bright
amongst rows of corn and beans and trees and hills,
the browns and yellows and prairie grasses.

She ate the crops so she had to be taken down.
Her feathers would be plucked for the millinery trade.
(It's all about fashion.)

When she shines so bright, she garners attention.
When she shines so bright, she becomes a target.

Chew On This

Sometimes one must become a man-eater to survive.

We have all heard about the quick decapitation of a male mantis—
when she is done sexing him, praying before she feasts on his body.

The female anaconda could not stand her smothering man—
she wrapped herself around him so tight he lost his breath.

The blue octopus did the same with her tentacles—
dragged him back to the cave, man. Seafood is on the menu tonight!

The male redback spider performs his best bedtime moves
before finishing with an acrobatic finale—

flying high up in the air, completing a fine double-flip,
before lowering himself into the gaping mouth of his mate.

Sometimes one becomes a man-eater.
Once a man tried to break me; I won't make that mistake again.

An American Metaphor

My phone autocorrected *decay* to *sexy*.
There's a poem there.
You write it.

IV.

Conversation with a Grandfather

I don't know where to place my anger, I apologize,
tightly clenching my toes and my fists beneath the table.

Never try to bury your anger, son.
That simply feeds the fury, he says.

But I think I will explode,
I reply.

Then let it out. You are allowed to erupt from time to time.
Sometimes brilliance comes from the flash.

Sump Pump

"Goddamn it!"

Kyle dropped his fork and winced, rubbing his forehead. *Here we go again*, he thought to himself.

Aida, his mother, jumped.

His baby sister, Sarah, began to cry.

"Shh," Aida said, rubbing Sarah's forearms, attempting to hush her. They didn't need any other reasons to irritate Carl. She hummed softly, and Sarah's crying slowed to a slight snivel. The baby picked up a piece of cereal.

Aida and Kyle returned to their pasta. They were going to get sick of pasta. And rice. And beans. But as they looked out at the rain, they knew that's what they'd be stuck with for a while. Carl was going to get sick of it even faster, but the road to the grocery store was probably washed out by now. They could call the emergency center to drone out some supplies, but Carl was too proud for any of that. *We don't need no fucking handouts. I can provide for us*, he would say.

They could hear Carl's boots stamping their way up the basement stairs. "The goddamn sump pump is broken."

"But this is going to be a twenty-day stretch," Aida stated.

"*This is going to be a twenty-day stretch*," Carl imitated Aida, mockingly. "No shit. Why do you think I'm so upset?" He lifted his hand as if to smack her.

Kyle sat up defensively, wide-eyed.

"Don't worry, *son*," Carl scoffed, laying his hand to rest. He turned to the sink to wash up, soaping up to the elbows, muttering to himself. "There's already almost a foot of water in the basement."

"What are we going to do?" Aida asked in a panic.

"*We?*" Carl replied. "*We* aren't going to do nothing. That's all *you* are good at—nothing. *I* will get my tools from the truck and work on it after I eat my damn dinner."

"Your plate's in the microwave, dear."

"It's cold."

"That's why it's in the microwave, dear."

"Your pasta isn't any good reheated," Carl complained, sitting down at the table with his plate.

Kyle watched as his father added way too much salt to his meal and overstuffed his mouth with large forkfuls of pasta. *Choke on it*, he wished.

After dinner, Carl did as he promised.

Aida gave a sigh of relief as he returned to his lair.

*

As Kyle descended the stairwell and into the living room, Aida looked up from her sewing long enough to sincerely thank him for putting his baby sister to bed.

"No problem, Mom."

Kyle sat down in the armchair closest to the window and looked out at the rain. He hated the rain. It meant isolation. No school. No work. No escape from this place. No escape from *him*.

He sighed and tapped the corner of the window until a screen popped up. He tapped until he found a show worth watching, plugged in the chair's headphones, and zoned out from his teenage misery.

*

A thunderclap rattled the window. Kyle awoke with a startle. The lights of the house flickered. He took off the headphones and got to his feet, stretching before making his way to the kitchen for a glass of water.

As he walked into the kitchen, he found his mother whimpering.

"Yeah, you aren't going to do that again, are you?" Carl asked, twisting Aida's arm.

"Stop it!" Kyle demanded, shoving his father away.

"Do you think you're a big man?" Carl stepped up to his son, chest puffed out. "Do you?!"

Kyle could smell the stink on Carl's breath, but he didn't waver.

"Come on, son. Show me what you got. Show me who's the alpha."

"I just wanted you to leave her alone," Kyle replied, attempting de-escalation.

"She's *my* wife, and you're *my* son, and I'll do what *I* want in *my* house." Carl poked Kyle in the chest. Hard.

"Stop it. *Please.*"

"You're a chicken shit." Sensing victory, Carl sneered. His chest deflated. "Go to your room."

Aida gave Kyle a reassuring glance.

He backed out of the room and headed upstairs.

Kyle checked on Sarah before taking a long shower and brushing his teeth. When he went to head to his room, he found his mother weeping on the stairwell.

"Mom?"

She didn't answer.

As he came toward her, he noticed fresh bruises on her arms. Her skirt ripped and disheveled. A purple welt on her thigh.

*

Carl cursed as he stood in three feet of water.

He gave up working on the sump pump for the night.

His boots stamped their way up the basement stairs.

He opened the door to the kitchen.

*

As the door from the basement opened, Kyle swung the frying pan, smacking Carl right on the side of the head.

"Who's the alpha now?" he asked.

Carl stumbled.

He fell partway down the stairs.

He groaned and collapsed.

*

In the morning, water was seeping into the kitchen from under the basement door.

Takeoff

Blue heron takes flight
—goat's beard fuzz takes to the breeze.
I want to fly free.

Returning

Can you look at a photograph
and tell the difference between a sunrise and a sunset?

Is one more beautiful than the other?

Is there not magic in the air
of both dusk and dawn?

*

We climb hills and mountains
to get closer to the sky,
to a god,
to the great mother.

Higher and higher we climb.
Higher and higher we search.

*

Sometimes when we go it alone,
we find clarity,
see that the sky is wide open possibility.

*

From time to time,
fog and mist and rainclouds
may blur our minds,

but weather will always clear.

*

Clouds can be wisping.

If you stare long enough,
they will carry away our fears—
made feather-light.

*

We will rebuild our sacred social circles,
find true companionship
in those that see our sunshine
beyond the storm clouds.

*

A gathering of earthlings
congregate at the sea to watch the sunset,
They give a collective *ah*
in awe and peaceful contentment
as our own star slips away beyond the horizon,
knowing that the streaks of finger-painted reds
are a sign of the sacred journey
—our birth and death and rebirth.

We will always return.

And the World Keeps
Crushing This Fragile Heart

The strongest of all
things are often worn down
by time and by pressure.

Water erodes rock
—winter's embrace softens pine
needles on the ground.

Hunger

The dog fighter
keeps his best pit in a small kennel,
gives the animal little water,
no food,
no stimulation
for up to a week before the next big fight.

Throw a small cube of steak in the ring,
and see how hunger makes one bare their teeth.

*

It's all a laughing matter
when Petruchio starves Katerina
in order to make her obedient,
to make her a good weak wife.

*

The elephant gets a peanut,
at least when she performs the way she is supposed to.
It's that or the switch so she carries the acrobats on her back
as she stands upon their stool.

They cheer when they see her smile,
but that's not really a smile on her face.
It's a hungry cry for freedom.

*

Candy and hollow threats
are used as a tool to stop the child
from throwing a tantrum in the store.

Be good, and I'll feed you, Sugar.

*

Hunger can be self-inflicted.

Depressed captive dolphins may refuse food,
bash their skulls against their concrete enclosures,
and when they have had enough,
they simply choose to breathe no more.

*

Hunger can be self-inflicted.

One day without food. Two days without food.
Give us control over our rotting shells.

Five days without food. I'm searching the mirror for a change.
Give me power in this wasting away.

A Song Unanswered

David Boynton recorded the last known birdcall
of the Kaua'i 'ō'ō species in 1987.

She was the native 'Ōhi'a,
prominent tree of strength and stability,
grown from fresh lava's soil,
producing flowers of fire,
reds and oranges and yellows to admire,
nectar for insects to thrive,
shelter for the bird's song,
roots to help nurture growth
of other flora.

He was the invasive strawberry guava.
He was pretty enough and filled with sweet juices,
but he made an alliance with the invasive wild pig
to spread his seed so he could grow hearty,
so he could overpower her.
His hunger is a weapon;
his control is not outwitted
by hunters nor pesticides
nor prayer.

The Kaua'i 'ō'ō,
a child orphaned.
The small bird
cries one last time
for comfort in the night,
but only the night's silence answers.

I Don't Know If It Makes Me Feel Better or Worse That We Aren't the Only Ones

"A prior history of suicide attempt is considered one of the most robust predictors of eventually completed suicide."
—*The American Journal of Psychiatry*

A newspaper once reported
a story about a dog who couldn't be saved
from its own grief.

The dog jumped off a cliff into the water.
A gallant passerby dived into the river's muddy waters
and rescued the poor dog.

The dog jumped again and again
only to be dragged back to the shore
over and over again.

Eventually, the stubborn distraught dog
walked over to the river's edge and collapsed,
his head in the water, successful at long last.

The Yangtze

River of pesticide runoff;
of cereal boxes, needles, and plastics;
of disposable ear plugs, fishing nets,
Styrofoam, and floppy discs.

River of plenty is now running out of life.
Some like it dirty, some like it rough,
but this place is too dirty for some,
so dirty the Chinese sturgeons won't even fuck.

River of porpoise without fins,
big smile, round body thought indestructible,
now running out of food like the baiji dolphin,
her sweet dead uncle.

River of purpose, home of the giant softshell turtles,
once viewed as holy figures, as divine deities.
There are only a few left, all thought to be male.
Corporate greed won't stop until they've killed the gods.

And He Said He Wouldn't Have a Gay Son

He wanted his gay son dead,
so he shot him in the heart with his antique rifle.

He cut his son into pieces and dispersed the parts
inside the bloating stomachs of roadkill along highways 3 and 20.

When the sheriff found a human eye, sea-green, in the buck's
    intestines,
the DNR launched an investigation.

They found more and more human remains,
and they thought the deer had become aggressive.

So hunting season started early, and there were no limits.
And he couldn't have been happier to empty his casings upon the
    rich Iowan soil.

The Last Night on Earth

The last beings on Earth gather around a fire and speak.
Any barriers of communication are broken.
What a lonely night it would be if they still pretended not to
    hear one another.

The human boldly states,
There must be a way out.

The eagle opens its beak,
Your fire falls from the sky, human.
There is only so far I can fly up
before my breath is taken.

The whale replies,
And your plastics and oils and hairsprays
have tainted the ocean, but still,
there is only so far I can dive.

The cockroach hisses,
My ancestors spoke of this day.
Everyone said we would make it.
I thought there would be more than just me.

The dog replies,
I never thought of this day.
I only ever lived in the moment.
I won't let tonight be any different.

Together, they sit in the silence of *this* moment,
waiting.

• • •

The Oracle

What do you think the
gods will create when this is
all gone? I ask her.

We have failed the test.
The gods won't create. They won't
make the same mistake.

Acknowledgments

Thank you to these literary journals who originally published versions of the following pieces, sometimes under different names:

Emerge Literary Journal: "Interloper"
Flyover Country: "Birds"
Idle Ink: "Blessing"
orangepeel: "A Song Unanswered"
The Orchards Poetry Journal: "Willful Ignorance"
Qwerty: "Willful Ignorance: A Gay Scavenger Hunt"
Rabid Oak: "Conversation with a Grandmother"
Ridgeline Review: "Chew on This"
Stonecoast Review: "Trophy"
Under a Warm Green Linden: "When She Shines"

"And He Said He Wouldn't Have a Gay Son," "Hunger," and "The Yangtze" first appeared in the anthology *Querencia Autumn 2022* published by Querencia Press.

"Hunted" first appeared in the author's chapbook *Artificial Sweetness* published by Finishing Line Press.

"The Oracle (I)" and "The Last Night on Earth" first appeared in the anthology *Mother Nature Burns* published by Sunday Mornings at the River.

Brandon, as always, *je t'aime.* ♥

Mom, Grandma, Grandma, Sammi, Claire, Carla, and all my wonderful friends and family who continue to shower me with support—I am forever grateful.

Aurora Bones, thank you for the influential workshops.

Thank you to Tommy Sheffield and Megan Merchant of Shiversong for providing your editing services.

Thank you to Eric Muhr and everyone at Fernwood Press for helping bring this collection to print.

About the Author

Charles K. Carter (they/he) is a queer poet from Iowa who currently lives in Oregon. They share their home with their artist husband and their spoiled pets. He enjoys film, yoga, and live music. Melissa Etheridge is their ultimate obsession. Carter holds an MFA in writing from Lindenwood University. His poems have appeared in numerous literary journals. They are the author of *The God of Lonliness* (Rebel Satori Press), *If the World Were a Quilt* (Kelsay Books) and *Read My Lips* (David Robert Books) as well as several chapbooks.

www.CKCpoetry.com

Title Index

W

First Line Index